Cats

Betty Locke

ALL ABOUT CATS

MY BELOVED FRIEND, CAT

It is said that while one may own a dog, one is owned by a cat.

A cat can be a cuddly, playfully entertaining, affectionate addition to a household but it joins the family on its own terms.

Whereas a dog, lacking all sense of decorum, might exuberantly lick you all over, a loving cat will exercise a degree of dignity.

Rudyard Kipling's charming story, The Cat that walked by himself illustrates this very well. For anyone who might have forgotten it, here it is in a nutshell.

THE CAT THAT WALKED BY HIMSELF

Back in the times when everything was wild, the woman took on the task of domesticating the wild creatures starting with man.

She found a nice clean dry cave in which to live and lighted a fire for warmth. She then carpeted the cave with sand and grass.

The delicious aroma of meat cooking first enticed the wild dog to investigate.

Wild dog invited wild cat to come along but Wild Cat declined saying,

"NO THANK YOU, FOR I AM THE CAT THAT WALKS BY HIMSELF AND ALL PLACES ARE ALIKE TO ME."

Cats   Page 4

THE CAT THAT WALKED BY HIMSELF

Cat nevertheless hid near the cave entrance and he heard the dog being enticed to stay and help the man with hunting in exchange for the cooked meat.

The cat said to himself,

"That is a very clever woman but she is not as clever as I am."

Next, the woman dried some grass so that it smelled like new mown hay. Wild horse went to investigate and he invited Wild Cat to come along. And again, Cat replied.

"NO THANK YOU. FOR I AM THE CAT WHO WALKS BY HIMSELF AND ALL PLACES ARE ALIKE TO ME."

The horse went to the cave alone and became enslaved allowing the man to ride on his back for the sake of the sweet smelling hay.

The Cat hiding nearby remarked again,

" That is a very clever woman but she is not as clever as I am."

The next wild animal to be domesticated was the cow. Again, Cat was invited to come along and he declined saying,

"NO THANK YOU, FOR I AM THE CAT WHO WALKS BY HIMSELF AND ALL PLACES ARE ALIKE TO ME."

Nevertheless he listened as the cow agreed to donate her milk for the sake of the sweet smelling hay.

"That," he said," is a very clever woman but she is not as clever as I am."

He then approached the woman requesting permission to enter the cave and sit by the cozy fire and drink the warm white milk.

The woman laughed and said, "Go back to the wild woods for we have no further need of friends or servants."

Cat said,

" I am not a friend and I am certainly not a servant. I am the Cat who walks by himself and I wish to come into your cave."

The woman said, "You are the Cat that walks by himself and all places are alike to you. You are neither a friend nor a servant. You said so yourself. Therefore go away and walk by yourself in all places alike."

The cunning Cat pretended to be sorry and said,

"May I never come into the cave? May I never sit by the warm fire? May I never drink the warm white milk? You are very wise and very beautiful. You should not be cruel to a poor Cat."

The woman replied, "I knew I was wise but I did not know I was beautiful. So for that I will make a bargain with you. If I ever say one word in your praise you may come into the cave.."

"And if you say two words in my praise?" said the Cat.

"I never shall," said the woman, "but if I do you may sit by the cozy fire in the cave."

"And if you say three words?" said the Cat

"I never shall,"she said, "but if I do then you may drink the warm white milk for ever and ever. "

Then the cat went far away and hid in the wet wild woods until the Woman had forgotten all about him. Only the upside down bat that hung inside the cave knew where to find the cat and he reported what was happening.

"There is a baby in the cave," said the bat. "He is new and pink and small and the woman is very fond of him."

"Ah," said the cat, " what is the baby fond of?"

Cats   Page 7

"He likes things that are soft and tickly. He is fond of being played with. He is fond of warm things to hold in his arms when he sleeps."

"Ah," said the Cat, "my time has come."

The baby was fussing as the woman tried to attend to her cooking chores.

Then the bat that hung inside the cave said to the woman "There is a wild thing from the wild woods playing most beautifully with your baby."

"A blessing on that wild thing whoever he may be," said the woman. " for I was busy this morning and he has done me a great service."

That very moment the dried horse skin that hung at the entrance fell down - whoosh!- because it remembered the bargain the woman had made with the Cat.

 The woman went to pick it up and- lo and behold - the Cat was sitting quite comfy inside the cave. The Cat said,

" You have spoken a word in my praise and now I can sit for ever and ever inside the cave."

The woman was angry with herself, and the baby started to cry and would not be hushed.

The Cat suggested that if the woman tie a strand of yarn to a shuttle and drag it across the floor that the baby will laugh as hard as he is now crying.

"I am at my wit's end," said the woman. " so I will do so. But if it works I will not thank you for it."

Then as the woman dragged the shuttle across the floor the Cat ran after it. He patted it with his paws and rolled head over heels, and tossed it backward over his shoulder and chased it between his legs, pretended to lose it and pounced on it again, until the baby was laughing harder than he had been crying. The baby scrambled after the Cat, frolicking all over the cave until he grew tired and settled down to sleep with the Cat in his arms.

"Now, " said the Cat, " I will sing a lullaby that will keep the baby asleep for an hour. Then he began to purr, loud and low, low and loud until the baby was fast asleep.

The woman smiled as she looked down upon the two of them and said, "That was wonderfully done. No question but you are very clever Cat."

At that very moment the fire came down in clouds of smoke because it remembered the bargain she had made with the Cat, and when it had cleared -lo and behold- the cat was sitting quite comfy close to the fire.

The woman was angry with herself and she let down her hair and started to make a magic that would prevent her from saying anything else to praise the Cat.

Then a small mouse ran across the floor and the Cat said, "Is that mouse part of your magic?"

"No indeed," said she hastily jumping up onto a footstool and braiding up her hair to prevent the mouse from running up it.

"Then the mouse will do me no harm if I eat it?" asked the Cat.

"No," said the woman, " eat it quickly and I will be ever grateful to you."

The Cat pounced and caught the mouse and the woman said, "A hundred thanks, Even dog cannot catch mice. You must be very wise."

At that moment the pot of milk by the fire cracked and broke into two pieces because it remembered the bargain the woman had made.

And when the woman jumped down from the stool-lo and behold- the Cat was lapping the milk from one of the broken pieces.

The woman laughed and poured a saucer of milk for the cat.

AND SO YOU SEE CAT BECAME DOMESTICATED BUT ON HIS OWN TERMS.

THE RELATIONSHIP BETWEEN HUMANS AND CATS

In the long span of human residence on earth, perhaps no creature has intrigued and perplexed us so much as the cat.
We are attracted by her neat good looks, put off by her independence, amused by her antics, made uneasy by her composure, flattered when she rubs against our leg, irked when she yawns in our face and ignores our commands.

We envy her ability to relax. We like her softness to the touch, enjoy hearing her purr. We are wary of her claws. We are uncomfortable being fixed by her unwavering stare and we hate her caterwauling on the back fence at night.

We are gratified when she kills rodents, outraged when she kills anything else, particularly birds.

At times in our walk through history mankind has found reason to worship the cat, and at times to persecute her almost to extinction.

Our ever active imagination has attributed to her, wrongly and unfairly, many of our own worst character traits, while begrudging her possession of that inalienable right we have always sought for ourselves — personal freedom.

All in all, it is an odd relationship that people have established with cat.

Toward no other domestic animal do we show such split feelings of admiration and resentment — which is some kind of a comment on man, for the cat is constant. She has always been CAT.

With the other beasts we have clustered about us, the situation is clear. Our appreciation of chicken, cow, sheep, pig and goat lies largely in the taste buds. With astonishingly little protest, these citizens have allowed themselves to become the prime source of protein in man's diet. Every once in a while man considers his firm muscles, rich blood and keen brain and is duly grateful to the various fricasseed, broiled and barbecued contributors to his condition.

But we wouldn't dream of changing the setup. For none of these barnyard friends really qualifies as a pet.

Cats

CAT'S RELATIONSHIP WITH MAN

Pharaoh's imperious manner is typical of feline aristocracy

Pharaoh

Their manifest destiny is to nourish the family of man and, incidentally, to become calfskin shoes, pigskin gloves, Angora sweaters, long woolen underwear, glue, fertilizer and other products of man's invention. Furthermore, one is a little loss to the world when one is considered chicken-hearted, or as blankly stupid as a cow, sheepish as a sheep, hoggish as a pig and lecherous as a goat.

The horse has fared slightly better. He has been held in high esteem because he is swift, durable and strong, and because man looks so majestic riding him. He is also teachable and obedient, two qualities man always has insisted on in animals who wish to be his friends. The horse, however, is passing from the scene. The machine age has diminished his value as a work animal; his centuries of service are commemorated solely in the horsepower rating given to the vehicles which have supplanted him.

Even riding is a declining art, practiced nowadays almost exclusively by jockeys, cowboys and debutantes.

Perhaps the horse's greatest failing has been his size. His permanent place as one of man's pets was lost the day it became clear he was too big to be a member of the household. Today he enters only in cans and packages, as dinner for dog and cat.

Pharaoh is very conscious of her royal lineage. She tolerates humans perhaps reluctantly. However, she will not jump through hoops for us. She will not fetch the newspaper or our slippers. She will not wag her tail for the sheer delight of being in our presence. Nevertheless she acknowledges the homage we pay her by purring and rubbing against our legs.

MAN'S RELATIONSHIP WITH DOG

BARON
Ever obliging

With the dog, man seems to have made his peace early. Man understands dog. He is comfortable with dog. He appreciates dog's loyalty, courage, intelligence and — again — obedience; particularly obedience, for however sentimentally men and dogs view their abiding friendship, it is not a relationship of equals.

Dog is essentially a servant. His feelings toward his master are comradely and his manner familiar; he enjoys the master's affection and regard. But *his* place was fixed long ago when man told him, "Don't call me. I'll call you."
Furthermore, since man always has had difficulty with foreign languages, the channels of communication have been a one-way street.

Dog has eagerly studied man-talk, and man, in his wisdom, has patiently taught dog the terms of his servitude —

"Baron, Sit!" "Baron, Fetch!" "Down sir! and "Stop that infernal barking!"

In accommodating himself to this design for living, dog has, of course, surrendered his pride. This is evident in, if not the cause of, such vulgarities as his graceless eating, loud breathing, poor grooming, pungent aroma and appalling bathroom habits, all of which characterize him as a good-natured slob.

Dog's sacrifice of his self-respect, however, is not unrewarded. Despite his slovenly nature, he has had the discernment, the fine discrimination, to idolize man, and man, who couldn't be more approving of the choice, has conferred nobility upon the dog.

Cats

MAN'S RELATIONSHIP WITH CAT

Mitzy

She knows her name and she will come if she feels like it.

The cat is different. She serves no one, knowingly or willingly.

Her one accomplishment — the hunting of mice, rats and other rodents — is self-taught.

The man does not live who can claim to have trained a cat to perform a task for human benefit.

For their own convenience cats have learned various small maneuvers, like opening doors, but they do not and will not herd sheep, carry messages or run back to the ranch seeking help for jammed-up cowboys.

There are no police cats, no watch cats, no sled cats.

The cat does not even come when she's called unless it suits her.

Stubborn independence in others often puts man's nose out of joint, and it was at such moments that he probably began comforting himself by maligning cat's character. She was sly, treacherous, cruel; you could never tell what she was thinking; but she sure looked as though she knew what people were thinking.

From here, of course, it was a short step to deciding that cats were the companions of witches and suffocated babies by sucking their breath.

Actually, if cats disliked people there would be no more sense in associating with them than with tigers.

Cats

The fact is that on certain terms, largely unpredictable, owing to the wide variety of feline temperaments, it is quite possible to develop a warm and lasting friendship.

This, too, may not be a relationship of equals — the matter of who has the upper hand will always be in doubt — but it must be based on the free choice of the principals, on a willingness to tolerate different social and cultural patterns, and on an honest respect for each one's individuality.

In this, the cat will come more than halfway. Once a cat has established rapport with you, she is anything but aloof — dignified and with a strong sense of privacy, yes; but withdrawn, disdainful, isolationist, no.

She will try very hard to teach you cat language, which is only fair and proper since she understands considerable man-talk, even though she is not often persuaded to heed it.

(Like humans, cats vary in talkativeness, so the amount of conversation you have with one is not necessarily a measure of your friendship.

Some cats reply to human remarks simply with expressive gestures — a flick of the tail, a blink of the eyes or sudden attention to a spot of fur which needs washing. It is never quite clear what any of this means.)

Cats are also quite self-sufficient. You never have to entertain them. This is not to say that they cannot be entertained or that they themselves are not entertaining. It is just that their errands are many and their schedules full.

Admittedly, many of a cat's waking hours are devoted to sleep, and a cat prowling purposefully through tall grass is often simply looking for a warm, safe place in the sun for a cat nap. But they do not moon and mope, like dogs, for the need of someone to do their thinking for them.

Cats generally have a good sense of fun, although they are too dignified to have a real sense of humor. And since they are eminently practical, their games are all variations on the skills and techniques of hunting. They will stalk, pounce upon and wrestle furiously with a string pulled tantalizingly across the rug; dance around a rolling marble and cuff it with their fore paws, as though it were a mouse; or sit behind a door, ready to slide a paw under it and snag any moving thing that comes within reach from the other side.

Cats   Page 14

In playing these games, cats will act the clown but never the stooge. They enjoy being laughed with but can't abide being laughed at, and will walk away stiff-legged if they are made to feel ridiculous.
Cats are very conservative creatures. They like to do things in their own way, within a familiar frame of reference.

Change often unsettles them, and no amount of human reassurance will make them feel the least bit better about it. They often hate traveling in cars or trains and will complain bitterly until the trip has ended.

They are suspicious of a new item in their diet or of a familiar one prepared differently, or served up in a new dish or in strange surroundings. This often is interpreted as contrariness. And, indeed, many of a cat's actions do seem quite perverse. She will sit in forbidden chairs at almost every opportunity, and depart immediately from any chair, or other perch, on which she is put. She will sit and blink at human invitations to come in or go out, and scratch at the door five minutes after you have given up in disgust, asking to come in or go out.

What we are dealing with here is simply the cat's monumental, stiff necked resistance to anything that is not her own idea. Occasionally she will seem to obey, but this is merely a happy coincidence of your wishes and her intentions. Don't be encouraged. Essentially, she bends her will to no one.

For man this is a quality both admirable and exasperating.

It requires courage and strength of character, yet it can be wearing to cope with. If your exasperation outweighs your admiration, there is no point in having a cat for a pet.

Cats   Page 15

SABRE TOOTHED TIGER

Astonishingly little is known about the history of the cat. While her path has paralleled man's for thousands of years, he has noted few milestones in their journey together.

For this it seems reasonable to blame the cat. Man has always been a fairly close observer of the world around him and an incurable diarist. If the ancestral cat does not appear in cave drawings or on clay tablets, it is very possibly because then, as now, she walked alone and seldom came when called. Out of sight, out of mind.

There is an Arab myth that the cat came into being on Noah's Ark when one of the two lions sneezed and the first feline leaped out of his nose. As myths go, this is plausible enough, except that there is no suggestion as to how the premier cat managed to perpetuate the race. Somewhat more scientific opinion holds that the cat became cat about 40 million years ago. She was not the cat we know today, but she was beginning to be. And she had already come a long way from her starting point: Miacis, a weasel-like creature of the Eocene epoch (40 to 60 million years ago), who is also responsible for bears, raccoons, hyenas, dogs (yet) and civets — an oddly assorted lot which is not even on speaking terms today.

Cats developed from the civet side of the family, and are also distant cousins of one of the most fearsome beasts of all time, the saber toothed tiger. Smilodon, the sabertooth, was a 14-foot engine of destruction with curving, six-inch fangs and a mean temper, who strode the earth for half a million years. Since he was padding around throughout the period in which the early apes learned to stand erect and become men, it is possible that he had much to do with the still-lingering human fear of cats.

IT STARTED IN EGYPT

The first tame cats of which anyone knows anything definite showed up in Egypt about 3000 B.C. They were descended from an African wild cat and were very much like today's house cat in size and proportion. They were short-haired and gray in color, with black stripes and spots on the body and legs. The Egyptians adored them and rarely, if ever, have cats had it so good again.

Cats   Page 16

The cats, as always, made friends first with the grain farmers, whose storehouses they protected from rats and mice. This service proved so valuable that eventually the cat was elevated to Egypt's large family of deities.

She became Pasht the Goddess of Light and was worshiped at temples built especially in her honor. (The Egyptian word "mau" means both 'cat' and 'light')

Cat holidays were celebrated with parades and revelry in the streets. Household cats were adorned with jeweled collars and earrings. Killing a cat became a crime punishable by death.
When a cat died it was embalmed, wrapped in burial cloths and buried in a special cat cemetery. Especially solicitous cat owners even embalmed a few mice so that Mau would not go hungry on her journey to the afterworld.

Cemeteries discovered by archeologists in the nineteenth century were found to contain hundreds of thousands of cat mummies. And this being a practical era, the mummies were promptly sold by the ton for use as fertilizer.

Cats   Page 17

The Egyptians' excessive admiration for the cat eventually played a part in Egypt's downfall.
It is said that when the Persian king, Cambyses,the son of Cyrus the Great, was besieging Pelusium in his classic invasion of Egypt, he threw live cats over the wall of the city.

This heartless hailstorm of sacred mousers sent the Egyptians into a panic, and while they were distracted and unnerved their stronghold was overrun.
Cats and conquerors have rarely got on well together, incidentally, and Cambyses was a typical tyrant in this regard.

It is probably too simple to say that mighty monarchs can't stand the cat's bland refusal to take any sort of loyalty or fealty oath, but the fact remains that Alexander the Great and Napoleon were cat-haters and that Louis XVI of France took part in celebrations whose high point was the torturing of cats by burning.

How and when cats spread around the world is a matter of conjecture. Apparently, however, their emigration from Egypt began shortly after the Egyptians made it illegal to export them.
Phoenician traders are sometimes credited with introducing cats to Italy. And undoubtedly pioneering cats began to jump ship at various ports as soon as their now-traditional friendship with sailors was established. In any event, the cat was known in Greece and Rome before the Christian era.
Once on the continent of Europe the Egyptian tabbies evidently mated with the European wild cat, and the progress of the race was assured.

The remains of cats have been found at Roman villas in Great Britain. By the fifth century A.D. the cat was comfortably situated in China, and in Scotland and the Netherlands.

Cats   Page 18

Rats and mice were a constant threat to food supplies and cats were valued for their ability to control rodent infestations.

By the seventh century, the Prophet Mohammed was renowned, among other things, for his fondness for cats, and the legend persists that he once cut the sleeve off a gown he wished to wear rather than disturb the cat sleeping on it.

By the tenth century the cat was everywhere and greatly esteemed. In Saxony, Henry the Fowler ruled that anyone who injured a cat should pay a heavy fine. An early Prince of Wales,, enacted laws which set rates and values for cats of various ages and rat catching abilities.

In the Far East those relentless borrowers, the Japanese, having already obtained their written language from China, added the cat to their list of imports. Mao, as the Chinese called her, was so rare and so expensive at first that the Japanese decided that a cat-killer and his family would live under a curse for seven generations.

It appeared that the peaceful, hard-working cat had found her place as man's ally in his endless battle against the marauding mouse and rat invasions.

CATS' GREAT FALL FROM FAVOR

Medieval man, however, whatever his glories, peered at his world through a fog of superstition. He believed that demons and witches walked abroad, and saw their evil hand at work in the misfortunes that befell him. He was also close enough to the earth to believe that nature was inhabited by spirits, hard to please and easy to offend, who could help or harm him. And so he built his cathedrals, aspiring to the one God for whom the new Church spoke, and feared the Devil's legions who showed themselves so often and in so many guises in his daily life.

The poor cat became regarded as the embodiment of evil!

In Europe man's ceaseless struggle with himself is often felt by innocent bystanders, including the cat which went from being an object of worship to a symbol of loathing.

In the German states particularly, cats became associated with Freya, the goddess of love and fertility — a sort of north country Venus — and a team of them was believed to haul her chariot around Valhalla. Obviously, whoever wove this little fable together had very little experience with cats.

Eventually the rites of the Freya worshippers became outrageous, and a wrathful church cracked down. In 1484 Pope Innocent VIII directed the Inquisition to burn the heretics as witches — and their cats. The human slaughter was appalling. In the sixteenth and seventeenth centuries, more than 100,000 witches were executed in Germany alone and another 75,000 in France. With them perished countless thousands of cats.

Cats

Once the cat was thought to have supernatural powers, no misfortune was too small to blame her for and no means was too severe to exterminate her. The folklore abounded with horror stories, bizarre, incredible and devoutly believed. The normal, night-prowling cat looking for mice became a witch, transformed by incantations to the Devil, and bent on evil errands. She soured milk, spoiled crops, brought illness, caused afflictions.

Many a cat was cruelly destroyed in the name of religion. It was a pious tribute to the church and a blow struck against the Devil.

The survival of the cat seems to have been due to her own resourcefulness and to the courage of her few remaining human friends. For it was literally worth a person's life to own a cat when the murderous frenzy was at its height. Old ladies in particular needed only to keep a cat to convict themselves of witchcraft.

The cat, especially the black cat became the embodiment of evil.

Millers and sailors stayed loyal to their small helpers, to some degree; some tough old dames managed to protect their hearth side companions; and writers and statesmen began to be numbered among the folks who traditionally and fundamentally liked cats.

Some of these, fortunately, were quite influential. The great political cardinals, Wolsey of England and Richelieu of France, both had a succession of pet cats and were neither bewitched nor bedeviled.

It is impossible to estimate how much this kind of support helped, but by the eighteenth century the tide had begun to turn once more in favor of the cat.

THE CAT IN AMERICA

The cat came to America with the colonists, and it seems fair to say that she contributed her share to the civilizing of the wilderness by her never ending war on rodents and vermin.

By World War II she was a well-established institution. There was hardly a single military base or depot which did not have its faithful mousers. She worked in factories and shipyards, in air and railroad terminals. Cats accepted for combat duty sailed with the Navy, flew with the Air Force and the Marines, and walked with the troops, who were, however, always described as dogfaces. Individual cats achieved fame by surviving long hours on a life raft after being torpedoed, by being enclosed in packing cases and surviving sea voyages halfway around the world, by being decorated for honorable service to the Allied cause.

In the war zones, of course, she again suffered enormous casualties and her greatest feat was in managing to survive there at all. At survival, to be sure, she has always been expert. She has seen to this by retaining the ability to forage for herself and for her young.

It may be less necessary for her to do so these days, but there are few cats foolish enough to forget how to do it. Experience has taught that there are few certainties in a man-sized world.

Serenely self-sufficient and magnificently independent, she can reflect — if she thinks about such things at all — that her lot generally has improved and is improving.   Her enemies actually are few and quite civilized. Aside from the people who "just don't like cats," there are some bird-lovers, some dog lovers, the sufferers from cat allergies and perhaps a few mouse-lovers.

Meanwhile, the ranks of her friends are growing.

Cats

The groups which historically have been her companions have been swelled by the tide that sweeps all before it: children.

And unofficial observation of suburban America suggests that many families which lack the acreage to keep a dog active and happy are acquiring and enjoying cats.

There is, of course, a large uncommitted population which doesn't dislike cats but doesn't like them, either. Perhaps the last vestiges of cat superstition are at work here. Old beliefs die hard, and there still are folks who will say that cats can read the human mind and see things invisible to man.

Our language, too, is filled with unfavorable references to cats which long usage has given the ring of truth. The catty person is spiteful and malicious. The cat's-paw is a dupe. The copycat appropriates others' ideas. To pussyfoot is to be evasive, indirect.

The catcall is derisive. Only the jazz world has cast a small affirmative vote by coining a term for the alert and knowing person: hep-cat. or cool cat.

Generalities — good or bad — have never impressed the cat, however.

She is an utter realist, no philosopher and very much a she. Considering the swaggering virility of the tomcat there may be room for argument here, but on balance it seems, in human eyes, that the feline personality is feminine. (Only the French, usually so perceptive in these matters, disagree. Le Chat is masculine.)

Like most females she is confident of her capacities and aware of her limits. She has no brag or bluster; she never overextends herself. Yet she faces life unflinchingly, knows what she wants and how much she is willing to put up with, or forgo, or insist on, to get it.

She is various. She is complex. She is intriguing. SHE IS CAT.

Cats
Page 23

In 1953 the American Can Company, which produced containers for commercial pet foods and was therefore interested, discovered in a survey that there were 26,700,000 domestic cats in the United States.

By "domestic" cats is meant cats who, however casual their membership, belong to human families.

Most of them — 13.2 million — were found to be farm cats. Seven million were city cats, and 6.5 million lived somewhere in between.

The South had the most cats (9.7 million), the Far West the fewest (3.2 million). The East had the most urban cats (2.4 million),

Warehouse Cats

The Midwest had the most farm cats (5.8 million); no surprises there.

Over-all, 29 per cent of the nation's families had one or more cats. Farm families had the most cats; nearly half of them owned three or more. The nationwide average was 2.21 cats per cat-owning family. Low-income families were found to be far more likely to have cats than were the high-income families.

To arrive at a figure for *all* the nation's cats, however, there must be added the worker types who patrol or inhabit our stores and factories, warehouses and wharves, restaurants and military bases, and who go down to the sea in ships. One estimate places them at half a million.

Then there are the cats nobody owns, who live a gypsy existence in the city streets and the wooded country areas. These may number another two million, although obviously a figure like this has to be either a wild guess or come straight from some cat.

Assuming the latter, we have a total of 29,200,000 cats, which is probably inexact and not highly important, yet rather nice to contemplate if you like cats.

HOW MANY BREEDS?

This great number makes rather impressive the fact that, despite the vast number, there are basically only two categories of cat: long-haired and short-haired. Within them there are perhaps six recognized breeds and several varieties about whose classification as breeds cat experts and fanciers have earnest, inconclusive discussions.

Beyond this, however, there is nothing more to choose from until you get to ocelots and jaguars. As a type, the cat has been remarkably consistent for a very long time.

In the cat world, as elsewhere, the common people far outnumber the aristocrats. It is a safe guess that 99 out of any 100 cats encountered will be plain, ordinary citizens belonging in the boundless company of Domestic Short-hairs. This is the proper name for the group carelessly called "alley cats," and while it does contain a number of woebegone and misbegotten creatures, it is not to be sneered at. It is a breed, and prime cats have emerged from it to win top prizes at cat shows.

The de luxe breeds in the remaining one per cent include the long haired Persians (and/or Angoras), and the short-haired Siamese, Burmese, Abyssinian and Manx. There are also several in-between groupings,such as the Blues and Tortoise-shells, which may be long- or short-haired and are classified primarily by color. The Blues, for instance, include the Maltese, Russian Blue, British Blue, and so on.

Persians

The long-hairs originally were called Angoras, after the Turkish city (now Ankara) in which Europeans apparently first encountered them. Actually, they seem to have been known in and imported from India and central Asia as well. People try to distinguish between the "true" Angora and the Persians generally, but the differences ,small to begin with, were further confused by interbreeding

THE PERSIANS
FELINE ROYALTY

Lordly arogance

The long-hair is enormously fluffy and can look haughtier than a Main Line dowager. But under the silky coat is a sturdy body and a warm heart. While long-hairs may seem languorous, they are cats first of all and entirely capable of the fun and games cats traditionally enjoy.   However, —they can be expensive to purchase. Sometimes anywhere from fifty to several hundred dollars for a superior one. Therefore many owners do not allow them to roam outdoors.

The long-hair is blockier in all dimensions than the short-hair- Its body, legs and tail are shorter, its chest and rump wider. The front legs should be shorter than the hind pair, and stand straight and firm. The head should be broader than the short-hair's, and the breadth accentuated by a short, pushed-in nose. The ears should sit on the side of the head and have a little tuft of fur at the point. The larger and rounder the eyes, the better. The fur should be long and glossy, with a luxurious ruff around the neck and on the chest, between the forelegs. The tail should have a tuft at the tip.

Cats

Long-hairs come in a wonderful array of colors: white, black, orange, cream, blue, smoke, silver, tortoise-shell and tabby. All the solid colors must be pure; the black mustn't have so much as a single white hair anywhere; the blue must be all blue — the whiskers and exposed skin, such as lips and pads of feet, as well as the fur.

The Persians in general can be intimidating. They seem to look down their noses at us with a supercilious air. We are left in no doubt that in their estimation we rank lower on the social scale..

Regal Disdain

HIMALAYAN COLOR POINT PERSIAN

Aristcratic Scorn

**Adorable
Persian kitten**

Perhaps most sensational, and generally in high fashion, is the silver, or chinchilla, Persian. The basic coat is pure snow white, with each hair tipped in black.

Hey, Hop to it Human--
My dish is empty!

DEFINITELY ROYALTY

Domestic Shorthair

ORANGE TABBY

This tabby is a wonderful ornament for a bath tub although he probably has no interest in trying it out.

The Domestic Short Hair is a popular household pet. The tortoise-shell is black, red and yellow.

The tabby, which may be long or short-haired, comes in a variety of types, each with rigidly specified markings. Whatever the color combination, the tabby should have a light ground color against which her stripes, spots and bars may be distinctly seen. The tabby, incidentally, may be male or female. Tabby is not short for Tabitha, the traditional name for females (as Tom is for males), but comes from Atab, a street in Baghdad famous for watered silks, which suggest the rich and intricate markings of the tabby cat.

Along with perfect color and markings, the de luxe cat must have eyes of an appropriate shade. Most desirable with white fur are blue eyes (although this triumph of breeding seems to leave most blue-eyed whites deaf as a post). The silver should have emerald-green. Most of the others should range from orange, or amber, to yellow.

Cats

SIAMESE

Most prevalent of the fancy short-hairs is the Siamese, which may once have been the sacred cat of Siam and is one of the common cats there today. It is strikingly handsome and extremely smart, and is a good companion.

It is too taut and restless to be very cuddly, but it is a great talker and a fine mouser.

The voice has a high-pitched Asian twang with just a suggestion of the jungle in it. If one finds the tone unpleasant, one had better not get a Siamese, for it will be heard unceasingly by all — especially when the female is in heat. The yowls of yearning sound rather as though the cat were being rent asunder.

The Siamese is small, lithe and neat. It is leaner than other cats, with long legs and tail, and a firm, muscular appearance that implies power. The head, too, is small, and of a more sharply defined wedge shape than is found in long-hairs or domestics. The eyes are almond-shaped, very blue and often crossed. This may be disconcerting but, in this breed, is not considered a fault. The tail may be kinked or curled, but this is, too, is a virtue in Oriental cats. The fur lies sleek and flat, and over the body it is a light fawn color. Legs, tail and the mask across the face should be a dark, chocolate color. This may also be described as a seal brown, and the cat whose "points" are so marked is a Seal Point Siamese. Some are a grayish white with blue points and are, of course, Blue Point Siamese. The greater the contrast between the colors of body and points, the better the cat is judged to be.

Siamese kittens

Cats

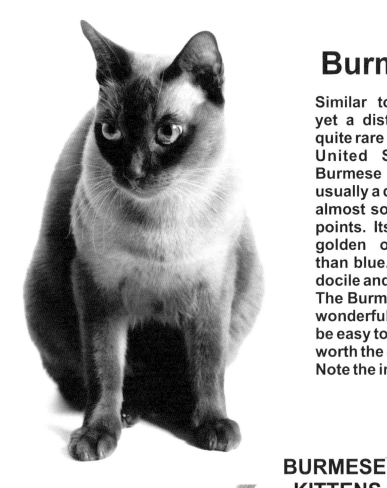

Burmese

Similar to the Siamese, yet a distinct breed and quite rare in the
United States, is the Burmese cat. Its coat is usually a dark brown, almost solid, and without points. Its eyes, too, are golden or hazel rather than blue. By nature, it is docile and friendly.
The Burmese cat makes a wonderful pet! It may not be easy to find one but it is worth the effort.
Note the intelligent eyes.

BURMESE KITTENS

So Cute!

Note the different shaped ears

Cats

Abyssinian

Also rare is the Abyssinian cat, which is believed to be in a direct line of descent from the famous cats of ancient Egypt.

It is a placid cat which talks little and has an affectionate nature. It is basically a shade of brown with variegated markings of black, gray or contrasting brown.
These should be definite, however, and not resemble the tabby. White spots of any sort are undesirable.

The Abyssinian makes a delightful pet if you are lucky enough to find one.

The Abyssinian has alert, relatively large pointed ears. The head is broad and moderately wedge shaped. Its eyes are almond shaped and colors range form gold, green, hazel or copper. The legs are slender in proportion to the body, with fine bone structure. It has a fairly long tail. The Abyssinian's nose and chin usually form a straight vertical line when viewed in profile. A m-shaped marking is often found in the fur on the forehead. This marking , also called " frown lines" appear above the Abyssinian's eyes. They can be colored ruddy, sorrel (red cinnamon) blue fawn or red. The Abyssinian is a medium sized cat.

Abyssinian kitten

Cats

Manx

Odd but not unusual is the tailless Manx cat, which comes from the Isle of Man, in the Irish Sea off the coast of northern England. Historically, the first Manx landed in 1588, when they deserted the sinking ships of the Spanish Armada. The sea-roving Spanish, in turn, appear to have picked them up during their travels from either Japan or the Asian continent.

The Manx is an energetic and resourceful cat which hunts not only rats and mice, but snakes as well. It is a courageous critter and fears no dog alive.

Part of its strength and speed comes from its curious build. Its forelegs are, ideally, very short and its hind legs long. This elevates the rump, which classically should be round as a ball, with a small dimple at the base of the spine where the tail begins in other cats. This results in a bobbing walk and a tendency to leap frequently while running.

The Manx does not hop like a rabbit, however, despite what has often been said by many people.

Manx kitten

Over-all, the Manx is small and compact. The ears are pointed. The fur is silky and comes in all the usual colors.

Taillessness, incidentally, is an uncertain characteristic. Manx kittens occasionally are born with tiny, rudimentary tails — which seems to disturb them not at all.

While Manx cats are generally tailless it should be mentioned that some Manx kittens are born with short little tails.

 Noted for being affectionate, loyal, and courageous, the tailless Manx is compactly built, with a rounded head; large, round eyes; and small, wide-set ears. The rump is also rounded and, because the hind legs are considerably longer than the forelegs, is distinctly higher than the shoulders. The Manx may be born with a tail but ideally the breed should be totally tailless with a hollow at the end of the backbone..

Cats

FELIX

Some years ago an elegant gentleman was part of our family. His name was Felix. Handsome in his black tux with white frilly shirt front he was a dandy figure of a cat. As an adorable kitten he'd had our complete devotion and as he became a refined and classy young tom cat we were eating out of the palm of his paw.

A remarkable distinguishing feature he possessed detracted from his charm not at all. He did in fact have odd eyes. Yes, one was gold color and one was green. We all worshiped him and he accepted the homage with feline grace.
One day however, he was inexplicably missing. Our children were devastated. Weeks went by and no effort was spared to locate him.

Newspaper ads, phone calls, tears and wailing were all to no avail. Months later we all sadly accepted that Felix was gone.
Then one day four months later, he came strolling nonchalantly up the driveway and walked into the house as if he had never left.
Would he be sick and emaciated? Was he in poor condition after fending for himself for so long? Not at all. He was the picture of health as he curled up his sleek well fed body on our favorite chair, purring contentedly. We rejoiced to have him home wondering where on earth he had been.

Three months later the whole fiasco was replayed. He went missing. We sought him frantically but lamented that this time, it was six months, he was probably gone for good. We were wrong about that however, he returned once more to take up residence with us, his faithful slaves.
About then, we had a visit from a lady collecting donations for charity She was sipping tea as we gathered our contributions when she exclaimed,

"My cat! You've got my Benny! I have been looking for him everywhere!"

"Your cat?" we protested, "that is *our* cat!"

"No," she said, "see he has odd eyes. It is my Benny all right."

She had found him utterly appealing on her door step, and 'adopted' him.

We did not have the heart to deprive her of 'Benny' so we continued to share him as he alternated between residences.

Cats   Page 35

THE BABIES

The cat begins life as an appealingly helpless little critter, blind, deaf and toothless. Its four inch body wears a first thin coat of fur, marked and colored in the pattern which will distinguish it as an adult.

Its sleeping kitten face is oddly like a tiger's, principally because the prominent ears are, at this stage, very small, rounded rather than pointed, and set far back on the head.

For the first few days of its life the kitten rests, bunched up, in the dim light of the nesting place, or crawls feebly among its fellows, conscious of nothing except its mother's warmth and the touch of the milk it eagerly and persistently sucks.

The kitten is soon able to smell and taste, and then hear. The eyes remain tightly closed however, sight is still a week or so away. The kitten eats and sleeps-a completely self-centered existence, warm, soft and nourishing.

The opening eyes are blank and blue, and will be highly sensitive to strong light for some days to come. As a rule the eyes open in anywhere from eight days to two weeks, and are adaptable to extremes of light and dark at a month or five weeks. But the timing in these developments is subtle and very much up to the individual. Once it can see, the kitten naturally seems perkier, although it actually is still very limited in its capacity to support itself and move around.

At a month the teeth begin to grow-a baby set which will be shed and replaced as in humans.

At the end of five weeks the kitten enters the stage at which its charm is quite irresistible, It stands, staunch and rubber-legged, peering at the gigantic world with round, blue button eyes. The inexperienced senses seek to translate the incredible events of each new day. The ears are up, the whiskers a-twitch, the ratty little tail held high.

The innocent face is humorous to look at. The erect, exclamatory eyebrows and often, the random accents of color create an expression of perpetual surprise. Altogether the kitten looks like a ferocious pansy.

THE BABIES GROW

A litter of these small clowns is great sport to watch. They are alert, lively and however their play may seem, seriously in training for the business of being cats. They wrestle mightily with each other, always seeking the underneath position and the opportunity of raking the enemy's unprotected belly with their powerful hind claws. They pounce on anything that moves intriguingly including mother cat's tail. They tussle, tumble and dance.

They dine ecstatically and sleep in a huddle. Perhaps most delightful are the infant approximations of big-cat behavior. Each tiny back arches at the threat of danger. A dreadful grimace twists the baby face and from the pink mouth issues a soft warning hiss, sounding very much like the exhalations of a steam iron.
Otherwise, for normal use, the voice of the kitten is high and squeaky sounding like 'eeee" or "eee-you."

Cats Page 37

Each day, each week, is one of achievement. At six weeks the teeth are in. By seven or eight unsteady legs are firm. By eight or nine the kittens are big enough to be weaned., although it may take a frightening, unexpected snarl from mother, or a cuff from her paw to convince them of it.

By now, too, they will have become distinct personalities. Or, at least, one will have asserted itself as boss of the litter, stronger, rougher, first at the dinner table, always at the center of the bed. Very likely, too, this is the one which will learn the most, and learn it most quickly.

Not at all sure about this new method of dining

Cats

Page 38

If it should become necessary a kitten can be hand fed using a child's toy baby feeding bottle. Watered down evaporated milk is best for this.

See, I can eat by myself, because I am a big cat now!

THE KITTEN GROWS UP

The kitten, of course, inevitably becomes cat and in the transition unfortunately loses its charm for some people. This is short-sighted in the extreme. For the young cat, sound in wind and limb, is about ready to enter a lifetime of service in the war on rodents, whether in the city or the country. (Not all cats- there are a very few exceptions, some shirkers. For reasons never satisfactorily explained, some cats, like some humans, never do a lick of work, although they dress well and are otherwise pleasant company. It is not necessarily a matter of home training, for other cats in the family may be excellent hunters. It may be that the gold bricks just don't like mice.)

At five months the kitten coat is shed and the coarser permanent fur comes in. The baby teeth usually go now, too (although maybe not until seven months,) and the business like adult set, numbering 28, appears. This includes 12 incisors (six each in the upper and lower jaws), four canines, eight pre-molars and four molars. The incisors bite food into manageable pieces for chewing by the molars. The canines, long and slightly curved, are available to deliver piercing bites to mouse or rat.

By eight months the female cat is physically mature, and in nine to twelve, the male. The kitten cuteness will have disappeared, but in its place will be the sleek efficiency of the young, wonderfully functional adult cat. From the tip of the sensitive stub nose to the tip of the flickering tail, she-or he-is a marvel of construction. The skeleton is engineered to bear the stresses and strains of all movements, whether they involve a powerful, spring-legged leap or a swivel of the head to wash a spot in the middle of the back.

Cats   Page   40

A cat is a wonderfully constructed. Its muscles are strung to allow great flexibility and agility. They are keenly responsive to the brain's command-as anyone knows who has watched a cat in pursuit of quarry or in flight from a dog. The curved, retractable claws, sheathed in repose, are capable of supporting the cat's weight in climbing or dealing a rakish slash to the body of an enemy. The skin is loose fitting, making it difficult for a foe to seize more than a mouthful of fur and giving the cat maneuverability to twist and turn, even when held.

The senses are acute, particularly those of sight and hearing.

This cat toys with object while hanging upside down

While cats cannot see in total darkness, they can see in better than humans in dim light because their pupils dilate more and thus make better use of the available illumination. They are also aided in seeing by their whiskers, which are not a measure of the cat's width, as is often thought, but serve as feelers in determining the shape and location of objects.

This cat twists his body in mid air

This cat plays with a dangling cord

CAT ON THE PROWL

By discovering a cat in various lairs, haunts and dens over a span of time, it is possible to construct a certain pattern of behavior, but you will never be sure. Completely futile, of course, is following to see where she goes. She will either go nowhere ore go somewhere. If she goes somewhere she is probably leading you to a place where she does not ordinarily go.

As far as anyone can say for sure cats like to rest under rose bushes, forsythia bushes or anywhere that smells sweet and offers concealment. There a cat can snooze, with ears a tilt for danger, and lounge seeing but unseen. The keen nosed dog will often pass within a foot and not notice the indolent cat. (This means that he knows she's there and doesn't care, or that he knows that she knows that he knows she is there and it is wiser to keep going. If he doesn't know she is there then he ought to see someone about his nose.)

THE CAT AS A HUNTER

Even in thickly settled communities there is a wide range of game for a cat. Aside from mice there are rats, squirrels, moles and other furry creatures. On the prowl her ears are attuned to the merest whispers of sound and the gentle tabby becomes a destroyer as fearsome as any of her wild cousins.

THE HUNT

Her cautious footfall is silent, her gaze alert, her proud tail is carried low. When the quarry comes into view she crouches, head out thrust, eyes level and intent. With infinite stealth she eases forward, acutely responsive to every attitude of vigilance or torpor in her prey. As she comes into range her chin juts out over evenly place front paws, her eyes are electric. Her hind legs are gathered under her, the muscles of her haunches flexing alternately as she seeks the ideal footing for the take off. Tension is drained off through the switching tail, leaving the body superbly poised, almost relaxed. The leap is high and short, a pounce which brings the front paws reaching forward, claws distended. The canines bite searching for spine or brain.

The kill may be swift or lingering. The killer toying with her victim is no spectacle for sentimentalists but in time the cat slays the mouse and gravely eats it.

Many cats, it should be mentioned, prefer to lay the mouse on the doorstep as a trophy, and all cats enjoy being praised for their accomplishments. There is of course, no use in placing a moral value on the performance. Nature permits many unequal struggles and miserable deaths, and so does man, who invented the SPCA in order to restrain himself.

A cat may be frightened or discouraged from hunting at all, but she will not change her techniques. About all the distressed human can do is not look, or dispatch the mouse himself, remembering that few mice are as pleasant or hygienic as Mr. Disney's.

By late afternoon the daytime cat usually returns from wherever she's been and checks in at home. She may scratch at the door or stand on a window sill to call attention to her arrival. Or perhaps she will sit on the porch, cleaning her fur and gazing at the world until noticed and invited in.

The aroma of family dinner cooking in the kitchen will set the cat to clamoring for her own, and after being fed she most likely will settle down for the evening.

She might be tempted to play with a string or a cat nip mouse, but the chances are that she will prefer to find a spot- under a lamp, or on top of a warm television set - in which to rest, relax and sleep. This is the time cats purr loudest.

Cats

CHOOSING A CAT

There are many ways of acquiring a cat, and most of them happen tomost people long before they ever think of going out and getting a cat in the proper manner.

The cat is a prolific creature, no question about it, and people whohave cats to begin with soon have extra cats. Few things in life are free,but kittens are one of them.

A cat-owner may even insist on paying you a fee to take a kitten off his hands!

This turn of events does not qualify, however, as choosing a cat. Nor does adopting a stray that comes to the door, or returning from the country vacation with one of the farmer's cats or helplessly accepting the bedraggled kitten found and brought home by one of your children.

Picking a cat assumes you have none and intend to keep it that way until you find *the* cat for *you.*

This means decisions: Breed? Male or female? And, perhaps, how many? Essentially, a cat does not ask for much, certainly not more than adult humans can provide. If you are prepared to feed, water and house it, and let it live normally enough to stay fit (and take it to a good vet when it's ailing), you rate having a cat —a Domestic Short-hair, anyway.

De luxe cats need more care, not because they're necessarily more tender, but simply to keep them de luxe. Long-hairs need constant grooming. Siamese kittens grow slowly and take watching. All purebreds require some exercise and yet probably shouldn't be allowed to roam the neighborhood to fight with or get pregnant by some low-brow. In short, you have to want a fancy cat, and know what you want.

If you are going to have your cat neutered it doesn't make much difference whether you choose a male or a female.

Cats   Page 44

The tough job of choosing a kitten
It ain't easy
THEY ARE ALL ADORABLE

Often as not a pair of attractively marked parents will produce babies with random spots and blotches—black eyes, striped noses, and so forth—that are most unbecoming. The same may be true of size and shape.

 A compact, neatly built mother cat may find her youngsters growing up to be thin-shanked, lean-bodied critters with no family resemblance at all.

If the owner likes cats impartially this will be no problem. Certainly it has never troubled cats. They are not self-conscious about aesthetic defects; none has ever felt out of place at a social gathering.

As a matter of fact, cats of all breeds always try to look as presentable as circumstances allow, and seem to have an eye for tasteful backgrounds— white bedspreads, red chairs, bouquets of flowers—which set them off to advantage. There may be other, simpler reasons for it, but there is no denying that cats have a sense of the dramatic. Every cat, whether a pure-bred Persian lolling on a silken pillow or a nameless waif resting beside an alley trash can, looks as though she expected to be looked at and, better still, admired.

Cats   Page 45

As for deciding between male and female, there's no choice if you intend having the cat neutered, which is operating to have the sexual function stilled. Otherwise, the tom can be a nuisance with his yowling, fighting, urine-spraying and other manifestations of the sex urge. And,of course, the female will present you every so often with kittens. At the same time, if you like cats you should permit yourself the pleasure of raising a litter.

How many cats to have is perhaps academic. As indicated, unless you take steps you'll eventually have a surplus, anyway. But assuming it is a matter of your choice, it might be well to consider how many you'd enjoy having around. Several are no more trouble than one if they've been kittens together. (Strange adults thrown together may be a different story.) But one is definitely less than several if you're the kind who dislikes reading the paper standing up because there's a cat in every chair.

Having decided, you are ready to confront a pack of kittens to choose.

If it's one of a kind you're after, you may have to locate a breeder and be prepared to pay handsomely. But if it's not too special an animal, most pet shops should be able to satisfy your needs at a modest price. And if, after all, you simply want a cat, there's always a neighbor swamped with a new litter. Just ask around.

So you look at kittens. If they're under five weeks, go away. They're too small to be separated from the mother cat, and you can't tell anything much about them as individuals. (You can tell they're old enough if the full set of baby teeth is in.)

At around five weeks, you're back. What do you look for?

YOU LOOK FOR THE ONE YOU LIKE BEST;
THE ONE THAT TAKES A SHINE TO YOU.

Cats   Page 46

PICKING A HEALTHY KITTEN

These kittens are fascinated with Mother's tail

Usually, what attracts you are the signs of a healthy kitten. The eyes will be blue and rather empty-looking —the kitten is still learning to use them properly — but they should be clear. The coat will be a downy, baby fuzz but it should be lively looking. Drab or patchy coats suggest that all may not be well.

As for color and markings, the baby coat is it. It may become more sharply defined as the cat matures., but it won't change — except with Siamese. In Siamese the light coat which is so desirable as a contrast to the chocolate points — or better still, the whitish ground color of the Blue Point — cannot be predicted with much accuracy from the appearance of the kitten.

One feature you can count on is the eyes: Siamese kittens' eyes are as blue as they will ever be.

The lightest kitten may not be the lightest cat. Use your own divining rod. The markings may be unclear on a kitten but will intensify on the cat.

The kitten that catches your eye will usually be an active one, a playful one, a perky and responsive one. At all events, steer clear of the inactive or skittish kits.

Determine sex. People sometimes find this difficult. In the female, the anus and the vulva, which are located under the tail, are close together — the one a spot, the other a small slit. In the male, the outlets appear as two spots farther apart.

You can't examine your kitten like a vet, but you can look for external signs of possible illness. After two months, the meals can be reduced to three a day, but quantities should be increased. The amount may vary, depending on the cat. Whatever keeps her in fine fettle is just right for her. If in doubt, consult your vet.

Avoid a kitten with a runny nose, a discolored mouth (it should be a baby pink) or a distended belly (it should be firm and round, but not bloated or slack).

Feel the body with the fingers for rashes or skin troubles. Note whether the ears are clean (they should be). Call the kitten to you (1) to see if it's bright enough to respond and (2) to test for deafness. If it passes these check points — and the majority will — you've picked yourself a cat.

Cats are not the least bit uncertain about their ability to take care of themselves. This, however, does not discourage the people with whom they live. By close observation of cat's habits and preferences they learn to do for cat many of the things cat ordinarily would do for herself. This is known as cat care.

Actually, of course, cat care harmonizes the mutual existence of cat and man and reduces the inconveniences of their relationship to a minimum. In the cities of the civilized world, which have a few natural accommodations for cats, these arrangements undoubtedly are beneficial and even necessary. But it is also true that the farther out into the country one goes, the less is cat care of real concern to cat or man. With the normal cat, man has to meet only a few basic situations.

First of all, the entrance of a new little cat into a household requires that the creature be made welcome. This is best done by appreciating that, to a kitten standing barely higher than your shoe tops, everything —beginning with you—seems of overwhelming size and potentially dangerous.

Since the cat has both curiosity and courage, she will make her adjustment and her peace with her environment. But you can help by being patient and gentle. Avoid the sudden swift gesture that startles.

Tone down the loud laugh. Let the kitten get used to you slowly. Keep petting and handling to a minimum at first. Kittens are fun to fondle, but it is literally possible to kill them with kindness. It is also a good idea to introduce the kitten to its new home one room at a time.

All this advice is not intended to restrict your pleasure. What is important is getting your association with your cat off to a good start.

YOUR BASIC DUTIES

Your first duty is to provide your cat with a bed. Her preferences are in accord with universal standards: it should be warm and dry, of comfortable size, bug-free and protected from drafts. There are plenty of places meeting these requirements admirably, even in a four-room apartment — bookshelves, the floor in front of the hot-air vent, the master's bed — but most folks feel better if they have provided their pet with a box of some sort. And most cats enjoy the cozy confinement of a box well enough to use it. Beyond this, whether the box or its lining is plain or fancy is a matter of individual taste—your taste, because the cat won't care.

The only other article of furniture an indoor cat needs is a pan. There are cats who, by some stroke of fate, have learned to use the human toilet, but yours probably isn't one of them. Buy a pan. Enameled metal is best and easiest to keep clean. It should be large enough for the cat to maneuver in comfortably, but the sides should be low. It should be kept in one location, and it may be filled with kitty litter, sand, shredded newspaper or sawdust.

A house-trained mother cat will teach her kittens to use the pan, but if you should by chance acquire one that never got the word, it is easy enough to set the kitten straight. First, show it the pan. Second, after each meal traipse the kitten over to the pan and keep it there—without using undue force, of course—until it performs. You will feel that you are devoting an awful lot of time to this chore, and so you are.

But very shortly you will be able to gauge when (it's usually under a half hour after the kitten has eaten) and for how long your assistance will be needed. Don't clean the pan until it has been used two or three times;

Eventually, a bright little cat will get the idea and trot to the pan of its own accord.
Cats are tidy creatures. When they have the opportunity to deal with matters in their own way, out-of-doors, they select a spot that offers some privacy, dig a small hole with their fore paws, eliminate and then neatly refill the hole.

Indoors, a cat will feel much better about using a pan if the sand or paper in it is ample for her to paw around and approximate her normal procedure.

In cleaning the pan use warm water and soap. Steer clear of powerful disinfectants. They are unpleasant and very often harmful to cats, and almost surely will persuade them never to use the pan again.

Bathing a cat is an experience to be avoided. Ordinarily, she is quite capable of bathing herself. The rough pink tongue does most of the job directly, and moistens the forepaw for cleaning the face and hard-to-reach spots behind the ears. Occasionally, however, owing to a skin irritation or other emergency problem, a bath may be prescribed. The water should be lukewarm and shallow, the soap mild and unmedicated (unless the vet says otherwise). Theoretically, the cat is placed in the water, thoroughly soaped (careful around the eyes!), spray-rinsed, wrapped in a towel and briskly rubbed until dry.

This is all easier said than done. Keep Polysporin handy —you will very likely end up with some long, red skin irritations of your own.

For all practical purposes, brushing a cat is the best way to assist her own efforts. Use a stiff-bristle brush — not wire — on her coat a few minutes each day. It will remove loose hair and dried skin, which not only makes kitty feel fine but keeps her from swallowing too much hair as she cleans herself. A good way to help short-haired cats get rid of loose hair is to wet the palm of your hand and stroke the cat about 50 times. The moisture will pick up the loose hairs. And cats won't object to it as they might a brush.

Most cats are playful and enjoy toys, which need not be numerous or elaborate. A catnip mouse or catnip-impregnated rubber ball are fun. Otherwise, a spool, or even a string with a twist of paper tied to one end, is enough to start a cat leaping, dancing and chasing.

Pipe cleaner

A simple scratching post is easily made from an 18" length of two by four or four by four attached to a weighted base. Cover the upright with an odd piece of carpet. Tack or glue into place securely. It is a good idea to tuck some catnip underneath it.

It offers kitty a chance to hone her claws a bit, which periodically she will want to do, without ruining the couch. Make sure the base is large enough so the contraption will not tip over.
Attach a pipe cleaner to the top. It will continue to quiver after the cat has touched it.

If you can afford it there are some elaborate scratching posts available on today's market. They are made in different sizes and shapes, some about four feet tall. They come complete with places to climb and nooks in which to hide.

If even with a scratching post, your kitten insists upon clawing the furniture, slap the palm of you hand sharply with a rolled up newspaper.

The noise will frighten her, and she should stop after a few repeat performances.

But you must catch her in the act each time. Cats and other pets associate noises with what is happening right now.

Cats

DOGS AND CATS

Despite the common belief that cats and dogs don't mix, Cats and dogs can and do become friends.

Cats who through some mischance have lost their kittens have been known to mother most unlikely small fry. such as chicks, ducklings, rabbits and even puppies.

What can be somewhat difficult, because it has not been arranged by the cat, is keeping alien pets together under the same roof. Usually this involves dog and cat, and the results are unpredictable, though successful often enough to be worth trying.

It's easiest, of course, to raise puppies and kittens together, as they have been on countless farms. Puppies, whatever problems they may have, are the soul of good fellowship, open, trusting, everybody's friend—which means that half the battle is won.

Kittens, if not mauled or frightened out of their wits, will spit their protests for a few days and then learn to live and let live.

The same pattern generally is followed when a kitten is introduced to a family's adult dog, although care must be taken that the canine, in a transport of joy, does not break his little playfellow's neck.

A much rougher situation arises when a defenseless puppy joins a household in which an adult cat is well entrenched and reigns supreme. It can be worked out, but you have to want a dog an awful lot.

In this case, or in the even more hopeless one of adult dog and adult cat, start by having your vet trim the cat's claws. This is trickier than it seems and should be professionally done.

Cats

As each new smell lingers and becomes familiar after a couple of days the animals will accept that they must belong. Familiarity, normality and habit all serve to break down the basic and traditional fears, hostilities and insecurities felt between species.

Let the first meeting be casual and brief. Stick around to see that a fight doesn't develop, but don't interfere any more than you have to. It figures that any show of favoritism will be deeply resented by the one left out, especially the cat.

A scolding of one in front of the other will be most mortifying, for the cat. If all goes well, cat and dog will begin eventually to exchange a friendly lick. When they nestle together for a snooze, play together and eat together (from separate dishes), love has triumphed.

Neutering

In every cat owner's life comes the time when the decision to interfere, or not, with the pet's sexual functions must be faced.

This is called "neutering," or "altering," or, more directly, castration in the case of the male and spaying in the female. Castration is surgical removal of the testicles. Spaying is removal of uterus and ovaries.

Both operations can be performed by a veterinarian with almost certain success, although spaying is more serious and the outcome will depend to some extent on the general good health of the cat. Recovery in either case usually takes about five days. And insist on an anesthetic. It's a lot easier on everyone, and will not add materially to the bill.

The arguments about neutering, pro and con, boil down essentially to two considerations: Do feline sexual habits bother you? Do you want kittens? These are yours to answer. Obviously cats aren't bothered, and apparently they want kittens. From a human standpoint, male cats are definitely milder if castrated and pretty obstreperous if they're not. In full possession of their powers, they fight and yowl and spray the premises with urine.

The real problem comes with the female. As noted elsewhere her sexual behavior is mostly embarrassing; her productivity, however, can be overwhelming. It often seems simpler to deprive her of the ability to have kittens than to go through the misery of disposing of her many litters.

Cats

If neutering is to be done, it's best done between six and eight months, although if you want your female to have a litter or two, it can be done later. Cats are such wonderful mothers, that it seems a shame to rob them of the opportunity to bear and raise kittens — at least once.

Don't worry about your cat's becoming slack or fat. This is still a matter of diet more than anything else. Nor will your cat lose the impulse or ability to hunt mice. There just won't be any tom catting, or any kittens.

unwanted kittens

The most humane way of (disposing of unwanted kittens is to take them from the mother as soon as possible after birth and have your vet or local ASPCA put them to sleep. If you wait until the mother cat has begun to get used to them and care for them, you'll have a mighty unhappy pet to account to for your heartlessness in breaking up the home.

Once the little family is established it's only fair to the mother to wait until weaning time, about eight weeks. Then ask your humane society to find the kittens a home or . . . well, look those babies straight in their faces and decide for yourself.

the old cat

Another painful moment comes when the well-loved pet reaches the end of its allotted span. Much as you may want to prolong an old association, it may be that illness or infirmity is making the cat's life difficult.

Each cat owner must choose for himself the best course to follow, but it should be known and understood that modern drugs are swift, painless and mercifully efficient.

feeding your cat

Feeding a cat properly is largely a matter of using good sense. What man has learned about the values of the food he eats applies pretty generally to cats, too. They need proteins, vitamins, minerals and the rest. Almost any food rich in these elements is good for the cat—if she likes it and doesn't have to eat too much to get the essential benefits.

This may horrify the purists. There are many cat owners and experts who supervise their animals' intake right down to the last drop of vitamin concentrate, and many who obey such long-standing taboos as no starches, no vegetables, no table scraps, and so on. This shows consideration for the cat and will do her no harm. Indeed, the majority of cats so fed are undoubtedly strong and healthy.

The point is, though, that successful results can also be achieved with less attention to detail and more to the general effect of your cat's diet on her appearance and vitality.

Cats   Page 54

A healthy cat is neither fat nor thin. Her eyes are bright, her fur is thick and shiny and she is as active as her age allows.

Some general points first

It's almost impossible to say how much or how often a cat should be fed. This must be worked out with the individual cat. Try only to avoid the extremes of over- and under feeding. This is not so easy as it sounds. Cats are interested in food and eating— No matter how well they may have dined, or how recently, they will sit staring wistfully whenever people eat. The temptation to share with them is strong, but resist it. It is NO favor to your cat to let her get fat and flabby from overeating.

At the same time, don't think that because she has caught a mouse she's through eating for the day. There is food value in all the creatures a cat catches, but in these civilized times it is difficult for her to snare enough of them to keep herself adequately fed. Remember, too, that hunting is hard work. No cat can do it well on an empty stomach.

Feed your cat at regular times each day, and keep her bowl in the same place. Serve her food at room temperature, and always keep fresh water available to her.

Cats have been known to like, and thrive on, so many unusual items that few foods can be ruled out absolutely. It seems to be agreed, though, that salted or spiced meats are not good; that pork in all its varieties is probably the least satisfactory meat; that a small amount of vegetables goes a long way; that any bone which splinters is deadly and must be avoided; and that candy and cake are less than ideal.

What's good? Practically anything else the cat will eat. Lean, raw meat is most attractive. Beef, lamb, veal, poultry are all dandy, if you can afford them. Horsemeat, frozen or canned, is just as healthy—and cheaper. Pork is possible, but should be cooked. Fish is fine, but it, too, should be cooked—and boned.

Perhaps more than anything else cats relish innards—liver, kidneys, heart, lung, gizzard. Unless you are a giblet fancier yourself, these items re a fairly inexpensive way to give your cat a de luxe diet without cutting into your own menu. Beef heart and lung, in particular, are pieces for which most butchers are willing to charge little or nothing. Also chicken heads—if you can stand them. Serve all of these things raw.

Cats   Page 55

FEEDING YOUR CAT

Probably the easiest way to feed your cat is with commercial pet foods. Some of these are dried and can be left in the bowl so that the cat can dine whenever it pleases. Some food are canned and they are fine too but must be refrigerated between meals. Choose a good brand of cat food and you can rest assured that the cat is getting all the nutrition it needs. You may have to discover which flavors your cat prefers. The main thing is to avoid monotony.

Your cat will need a raw egg two or three times a week to brighten up her fur

Occasionally green vegetables mixed in with her food is good.

Half a clove of mashed garlic to eliminate worms and a little mineral oil to help prevent the formation of hair balls in the stomach is a good idea.

Milk is not necessary and some cats won't touch it.

Cats

FEEDING THE KITTENS

The feeding of kittens is a little more complicated, mostly because attention must be paid to the frequency and amount of their meals.

The mother cat normally does the job very nicely for the first month.

Your only contribution will be to see that she is herself well fed, both during pregnancy and after the young ones have arrived. She will need bone-building calcium and muscle-building proteins in particular, and more water than usual while she is nursing.

If her milk supply seems insufficient you can supplement the kittens' diet with a small amount of slightly warmed, watered-down milk (unsweetened evaporated milk is easier to digest than milk with a high fat content).

By the time kittens are a month old they can begin to eat solids. Eggs, milk, fine-ground beef or horsemeat, or the various human baby foods containing meat are ideal for small, growing cats. It's also not too early to start introducing them to garlic.

Up to two months, the kittens should eat about four meals a day, at regular intervals. Quantities are small—perhaps a tablespoon of meat or half a jar of baby food at each meal, plus a shot or two of milk or milk egg mixture.

Cats

SICKNESS AND HEALTH

Given decent food and shelter, most cats stay healthy most of the time. Like any creature, however, they will have their share of minor ailments, and occasionally they are hit by a major disorder. The former you may be able to do something about.

The latter is definitely best left to a veterinarian. Most devastating—but easiest to prevent—is infectious enteritis, or feline distemper, a virus disease which has for years been the great killer of cats. There is now a serum which gives immunity, and there is no reason for not inoculating kittens as soon as possible after it is six weeks old. Enteritis strikes so fast and so mercilessly that there may be no time to act after the cat is sick. Also have your cat inoculated against rabies. This is not a common cat illness, but it is one that can be passed on to humans.

Perhaps the most usual health problem is worms. The cat with worms becomes a seedy critter. Its coat is poor, its appetite either ravenous or almost totally lacking. There are many varieties—roundworms, hookworms, tapeworms—and cats can get all of them. Some of these parasites are caught from lice or fleas, which even the nicest cat can pick up almost any time she is let out of the house. Others are carried in the organs of the rodents the cat eats. Usually, the cat ingests the eggs of the parasite, which then mature and fasten themselves to the intestinal walls. There they fatten themselves at the expense of the cat.

As noted in the preceding section on feeding, a small amount of garlic, taken regularly, is the simple way to guard against worms. Garlic will also work after a cat gets worms, although it's slow and a visit to the vet for de-worming would probably be better.

Fleas and lice, as well as parasites, may be carriers of diseases. To get rid of the wretched things, it's wise to dust your cat's coat, as well as brush it, every so often. Again, ask the vet for a safe powder to use.

Another common problem is the hairball. This is formed in the stomach from hairs which the cat has swallowed while cleaning herself.

Usually the hairs are eliminated through the bowels or by vomiting. But if they accumulate, they can seriously clog the stomach or intestinal tract. A small quantity of mineral oil or milk of magnesia is the best aid in preventing hairballs.

A real blockage is a serious matter and a vet should be called.

Chemicals in everyday use which might be safe for humans or dogs, but absolutely deadly to cats. . Or, perhaps more practical, keep your cat away from areas in which you've had to use these bleaches and other kitchen items

Don't use dog medicines on cats.

Don't use human medicines, particularly strong laxatives, on cats.

the medicine cabinet

Remember, whatever medication you use externally will be promptly licked off by the cat. It's got to be safe, therefore, as well as effective.

Perversely, of course, the cat will resist taking medicines for internal use.

There are ways and means of getting around her, though — aside from merely smearing it on her.

If the vet has prescribed a pill, try rolling it up in a patty of ground meat and serving it for dinner. If that doesn't work, or if the medicine must be given immediately, hold the cat firmly—to avoid being scratched, it's a good idea to wrap her in a towel—and press a thumb and finger on either side of her jaw to open the mouth. Drop the pellet in, hold the mouth closed and stroke the throat to encourage swallowing.

With liquid medicines it sometimes happens that a cat will simply lap it up from her dish. If not, finger pressure on the face will form a pouch in one cheek. Pour the medicine in. Don't try to open the jaws—the cat will do that as soon as there is something in the cheek to swallow.

Cats

A healthy cat
bright eyes
shiny coat

Give liquid medicine a little at a time, and hold the cat horizontal, which is her normal swallowing position. Anything poured straight down her gullet may get into the windpipe and choke her.

The main point is to be patient and gentle, independent soul that she is, the cat will not necessarily behave well and take her medicine like a little soldier simply because you are nice to her, But roughness or impatience will frighten her

SIGNS OF TROUBLE

It's too much to expect that we can learn enough veterinary medicine to spot accurately all the troubles your cat may encounter. There are far more of them, far more complex, than the few situations described here. Almost anything that hits a cat adversely, however, is reflected in a few basic symptoms that any cat owner can recognize. If you pay reasonably close attention to your cat, you should be able to tell fairly quickly whether she's up to snuff or below par.

HERE ARE CLUES TO LOOK FOR:

A coarse, dull coat, or one that sheds heavily and begins to look patchy.
Sluggish behavior and loss of appetite for several meals in a row.

Diarrhea.
Any swelling or lumps which can be felt in or on the body, particularly if there is any indication of growth.

Repeated coughing or vomiting.

Cats

THE VET

In so far as possible, pick your veterinarian the way you would a doctor for yourself. Look for someone of acknowledged medical skill, who inspires confidence and whose fees seem reasonable. You may not have a wide selection, since veterinarians are distributed rather more thinly than M.D.'s. Nevertheless, there should be one or two near you.

A veterinarian may be great with horse or dogs but he or she may not be so great with cats.

It must also be understood that cats are difficult to treat. As any cat owner knows, they put up a terrific fight against restraint, against medication, against undignified handling of any sort. They don't like strange places and are suspicious of strange people. Often they don't like traveling.

Put all these together and you have a fine description of a trip to the vet's to see what ails kitty.

She will be alarmed by the dogs in the doctor's waiting room. She will dig her claws deep to climb out of any arms that try to hold her. She will lick off her medicines, spit out her pills, rip and tear at bandages and stitches. And she will dislike staying in a little cage at the pet hospital.

If she is in for surgery, she: can be knocked out—struggling to the end —with an anesthetic, yet even then she presents problems. Being much smaller than most dogs, she gives the doctor very little room to work in and requires that he be especially dextrous and nimble in operating.

Cats

All of this is reflected in the attitude some veterinarians take toward cats.

What it all boils down to is that one should think ahead and find a suitable vet in case of need. You don't want to be frantically searching in an emergency

Whether the fees are reasonable is something you will have to decide for yourself.

Finally, if you're settled on a veterinarian follow his instructions faithfully and don't try to second-guess him. You can change to another doctor if you have reason to be dissatisfied, but while you're using his services don't try to pretend you know more than he or she does.

Human beings, being human, have been known to give up on a regimen of cat care — because it's too difficult to give the cat medicine, or to get a stool specimen, or to keep her confined — and then blame the veterinarian when there's no improvement in the cat's condition.

The four basic points in any relationship with a veterinarian are:
1. Satisfy yourself that you've got a good man or woman. .
2. Keep your cat healthy, but be alert for signs of trouble.
3. Don't try to diagnose illness; for yourself. Get professional help.
4. Always follow the veterinarian's instructions to the letter.

Cats   Page 62

THE FLAWS

The flaws in her character and behavior are actually inherent in being a cat and annoy only humans. These are her, or his, urgent and unabashed sexual performances and the howling attendant on them; the tormenting of captive rodents and the inability to distinguish between the songbirds that man cherishes (good birds) and the others (unimportant birds)

In suburbia, the cat's daily life is variable and unplanned. She lives in the present and there seems to be some scientific doubt about her ability to think in an organized way, to anticipate the future, or remember much of the past.

There are, first of all, two basic kinds of cat days: those in which she sleeps or lazes around during daylight and gallivants at night, and those in which she sleeps at night and cruises by day. The activities are much the same in either case, although hunting is usually better at night and human hazards, such as annihilation by automobiles, worse by day.

The day-shift cat rises with her humans. She arches, yawns, stretches and looks bleakly at the morning. Usually she washes and trots to the kitchen to ask what's for breakfast. A normal cat with a healthy appetite will have a great deal to say about this, most of it arguments in support of her being served first. There will be some ardent rubbing against a leg—table, chair or human—to indicate sincerity. And if all else fails, there may be some clawing at the upholstery, or other deliberate wickedness, to attract attention.

Cats   Page 63

CHILDREN AND CATS

Although families that have children do not necessarily have cats, most families that have cats also have children. This nugget of fact was discovered by the survey mentioned earlier and was offered without further comment.

This leaves up in the air a number of questions about the relationship of kids and cats, which is easy enough to observe, yet difficult to interpret.

Two facts stymie the adult in such research: he has never learned to talk cat and he has forgotten how to talk child. He communicates poorly with both his sources, therefore, and has to call on his mature reasoning, a poor substitute, to explain the obvious.

Adults want to know, for instance, why the cat which walks haughtily away when a friendly adult merely wants to pet it will submit to being dragged around by the tail by a three-year-old. The answer to this is so simple as to be laughable.

And so we come to the next point: kittens. Kittens, considering their pounds and inches, are very enduring. Not all of them, it must be said, will put up with the tail-dragging nonsense, but few will make a fuss as long as there's an escape route or hiding place available when things get too rough. This is because, as is well known, there is a secret alliance among young creatures, regardless of species. They may grow up to dislike each other, but while they are little and new they are *simpatico.*
Which is not to say that the young are more stable emotionally than their elders, but simply that they sense the youth in each other and are perhaps more forgiving.

This understanding between children and cats (or other pets, for that matter) makes it difficult to tell either the way to get on with the other. Mother cats, in any event., probably pass the word along to kittens. And parents just have to do the best they can with children.

Cats   Page 64

Since even the smallest youngster is larger than a cat, the responsibility for keeping the relationship nice and easy rests largely with him or her.

The cat's contribution will be extreme forbearance, no mean use of fang or claw and no bearing of grudges. On this basis, fine play is possible. The cat can learn to enjoy any game in which she is a participant, not a victim.

The hardest thing the child will learn is that the cat is most entertaining when given the freedom to be herself, least so when forced into someone else's pattern.

There are also times, it will be seen, when the cat needs to be left alone: when she's eating, for one; when she breaks off play, for another.

These, fortunately, are followed by times when the cat invites companionship or cuddling.

There is deep satisfaction for child or adult to have a purring cat pick his lap to curl up in.

Opportunities to return this regard will be many. For all their cleverness, cats cannot unlock a door, turn the faucet for a drink of water or ladle out their own food for dinner. Most children are pleased to be able to do so, and to help a friend.

It is useful to know how to pick up a cat properly: one hand holding the back paws and serving as secure support for the hindquarters, the other cradling the chest, in back of the fore paws. And never pick her up by the scruff of the neck. Cats soon become too big to have their weight suspended that way. Also, it's undignified to dangle.

For many children it is instructive to see how the mother cat bears her kittens, and how faithfully she raises them.

Cats

THE TWILIGHT YEARS

Throughout the seasons of the years this will be the pattern of her life-countless catnaps in the sun; countless mice slain and devoured;
as many kittens as nature and her human friends allow.
In summer she will enjoy the lush fullness of the earth, watching with eye and ear the movement of the days, and patrolling the scented
nights. The crispness of autumn will find her vigorously campaigning
among the harvesting field mice and southward-flying birds.

Her coat will thicken against the threat of cold ahead. On frosty mornings she will huddle in the pale sun, arising ever more stiffly as her years advance. In winter she will retire, a fireside cat, saving of the world's warmth that comes her way, cowering before the bleak winds, reluctant in the snow, slowed down and waiting.

With all other living things she responds at last to spring. The heart rejoices, the earth turns green, the air is filled with promise, and even old cats roll in the new grass, dance the skittering steps they learned as kittens and climb a few feet up a few good trees.

To every cat at one of these time spans will come the day that is the end of everything. With luck, the cat will be properly old yet free of disability and pain. With luck, she — or he — will have lived fully, known the urgent, purposeful mating with tom or queen, and passed on the natural faculties of being cat to younger generations.

With luck, too, she will have moved among people who cherished her, often for things she was not, but inescapably for the many honest things she was.

And for having shared her good life, they will account themselves lucky.

Cats   Page 66

DICK WHITTINGTON
Another famous cat story

Young Dick Whittington was left an orphan unexpectedly. His parents had been poor and all he had to call his own was his name and Mr. Sheridan, his cat.

His father had been employed by the local blacksmith to operate the bellows for very meager wages. Dick applied for the job that his father had vacated but the blacksmith hired someone else.

Unable to pay rent on the family cottage Dick was forced out into the world with nothing but the clothes on his back and his beloved cat.

They were often cold and hungry. Sometimes Dick found temporary work such as sweeping the steps of wealthy homes and he would receive just enough compensation to feed himself and Mr. Sheridan for a few days.

Work was scarce and Dick and the cat were munching the last of the food they had, when they were approached by a poor man begging for a bite.

Kind hearted Dick shared what he had and the man thanked him and then he said,

"How come a young fellow like you doesn't head for London?"

"London,? " asked Dick, "Why?"

"Because, young fellow, it is a well known fact that the streets of London are paved with gold."

"Really," said Dick, "in that case why don't you head for London?"

"I am old and my bones ache. It is about thirty miles away. I could never stand the journey. But if I was young like you I would go for sure."

Dick and Mr. Sheridan headed for London on foot. They searched the streets of London but they found no gold and not much in the way of work either. He found Londoners less than kind and sadly he wrapped up what food he had managed to scrounge in a large scarf and he and his faithful companion left London. They were a few miles out of the city when they rested very discouraged by the roadside. They had run out of food and as Dick sat trying to decide what to do the bells of London began to toll.

Cats   Page 68

The great bell of Bow rang out,

DING! DONG! DING! DONG !

DING DONG DING DONG!

Dick listened miserably and Mr. Sheridan rubbed against him in an attempt at consolation. Then as Dick listened, he thought he heard words accompanying the DING DONG.

The great Bow bell rang out
"Turn again Whittington, TURN AGAIN WHITTINGTON

THOU WORTHY CITIZEN

LORD MAYOR OF LONDON."

Dick and Mr. Sheridan resolutely headed back toward London

When they got there the streets were crowded. It seemed that the Mayor had been forced out of his mansion by rats. It was unbearable and many families were living in tents because it was not safe to venture inside their homes.

Dick told the Mayor not to worry and that he would help solve the problem.

"Your Worship," said Dick, "Mr. Sheridan will soon make short work of the rats."

The Mayor had his doubts. He said, "I don't think that cat can catch all of those rats."

But Dick and Mr. Sheridan went into the Mayoral home. The very presence of the big black cat was enough to frighten the rats and they fled in terror never to return.

Then Dick and his faithful friend Mr. Sheridan went from home to home to drive out the pesky rodents.

Cats

The Mayor was so grateful that he gave Dick and Mr. Sheridan accommodation in the Mayoral mansion.

The fame of Dick Whittington and his wonderful cat spread far and wide. Eventually Dick became Lord Mayor of London not once, not twice but THREE times in succession.

His Worship
Richard Whittington

Lord Mayor of London

Cats

Page 70

Made in the USA
Charleston, SC
28 September 2011